Enrich Bo

Grade 2

PROVIDES   Daily Enrichment Activities

 HOUGHTON MIFFLIN HARCOURT

Contents

BIG IDEA 1: Number and Place Value
Chapter 1: Number Concepts

Chapter 2: Numbers to 1,000

BIG IDEA 2: Addition, Subtraction, Multiplication, and Data
Chapter 3: Basic Facts and Relationships

Chapter 4: 2-Digit Addition

Chapter 5: 2-Digit Subtraction

Chapter 6: Data

Chapter 7: 3-Digit Addition and Subtraction

Chapter 8: Multiplication Concepts

BIG IDEA 3: Measurement and Geometry

Chapter 9: Length

Chapter 10: Weight, Mass, and Capacity

Chapter 11: Money and Time

Chapter 12: Geometry and Patterns

Pencil Place Value

Each pencil box holds ten pencils.
There are also single pencils.
Write the number of pencils in each row.

1. _____

2. _____

3. _____

4. _____

5. _____

Writing and Reasoning Which pictures tell you what the digit in the tens place should be? Explain.

_____

_____

_____

Expanding Numbers

Write the number. Describe it in another way.
Draw quick pictures to show the number.
The first one is started for you.

1.	<u>68</u>	<u>6</u> tens <u>8</u> ones _____ + _____
2.	_____	_____ + _____ <u>2</u> tens <u>3</u> ones
3.	_____	<u>90</u> + <u>7</u> _____ tens _____ ones
4.	_____	<u>4</u> tens _____ ones _____ + <u>2</u>

Writing and Reasoning Write the number 34 and the number 43 as tens plus ones. Describe how they are different.

_____

_____

_____

Name _____

Race to Find the Number

Draw a bicycle next to each helmet. Near
each bicycle, write the correct 2-digit
number. Then write each number another way.

1.

2.

3.

4.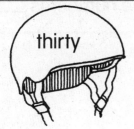

 Writing and Reasoning How did you choose
another way to write the number in Exercise 2?

_____

_____

Marble Match

Read the clue on the marble jar. Think of a
2-digit number that matches the clue. Write
the number as tens and ones. Write the number.

1.
More
than
46

_____ tens _____ ones   The number is _____.

2.
Less
than
70

_____ tens _____ ones   The number is _____.

3.
Less
than
95

_____ tens _____ ones   The number is _____.

4.
More
than
53

_____ tens _____ ones   The number is _____.

Writing and Reasoning Why do both ways
of writing the number describe the same number?

_____

_____

Name _____

Too Many Ones

Cindy made the sets of buttons below.

Make a new set for each amount of buttons. Use the greatest number of groups of 10 buttons and the least number of single buttons that you can.

	One way:	Another way:
1.	4 groups of 10 buttons and 25 single buttons	_____ groups of 10 buttons and _____ single buttons
2.	2 groups of 10 buttons and 34 single buttons	_____ groups of 10 buttons and _____ single buttons
3.	3 groups of 10 buttons and 47 single buttons	_____ groups of 10 buttons and _____ single buttons

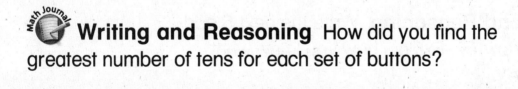 **Writing and Reasoning** How did you find the greatest number of tens for each set of buttons?

_____

_____

_____

Connect the Dots

Start at 1 and connect all of the odd numbers in order from least to greatest. Then start at 2 and connect all of the even numbers the same way.

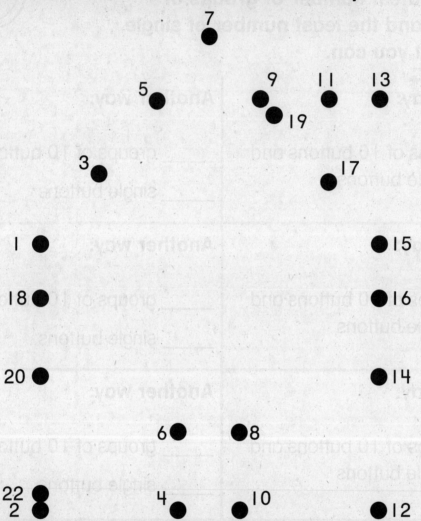

Writing and Reasoning Write the next 5 odd numbers that follow 19. Explain how you knew what numbers to write.

_____

_____

_____

Name _____

Compare the Scores

Some friends played a game after school. The chart shows each child's score.

Child	Score
Rosa	85
Eric	81
Dave	90
Gwen	78

1. Write a number that is less than Dave's score and a number that is greater than Dave's score.

    _____ < 90 < _____

2. Write a number that is greater than Gwen's score and a number that is less than Gwen's score.

    _____ > 78 > _____

3. Write the children's scores in order from least to greatest.

    _____ < _____ < _____ < _____

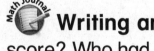 **Writing and Reasoning** Who had the highest score? Who had the lowest score? Explain.

_____

_____

_____

Name _____

Which One Does Not Belong?

Cross out the one that does not have the same value.

I. I hundred

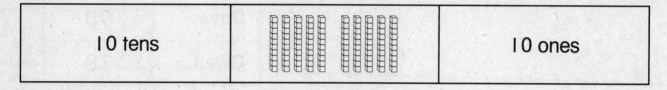

| 10 tens | | 10 ones |

2. I hundred 3 tens

| 13 tens | 13 hundreds | |

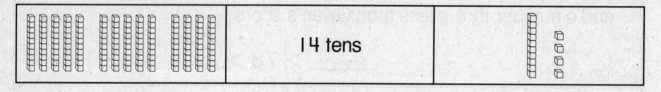

3. I hundred 4 tens

| | 14 tens | |

4. I hundred 2 tens

| | 21 tens | 12 tens |

Writing and Reasoning Explain why 17 tens and 1 hundred 7 tens have the same value.

_____

_____

_____

Name _____

Missing Pictures

**Each quick picture needs to be finished.
Draw the missing hundreds, tens, and ones.**

1. 354

2. 253

3. 216

4. 314

5. 264

6. 284

 Writing and Reasoning How did you decide
what to draw for Exercise 6?

_____

_____

_____

Name _____

Find the Number

Read the clue. Find the number.

1. A number is 4 hundreds more than 142. What is the number?

   <u>542</u>

2. A number is 2 hundreds more than 355. What is the number?

   _____

3. A number is 3 tens more than 249. What is the number?

   _____

4. A number is 7 tens more than 624. What is the number?

   _____

5. A number is 8 ones more than 331. What is the number?

   _____

6. A number is 4 hundreds more than 399. What is the number?

   _____

7. A number is 2 tens more than 923. What is the number?

   _____

8. A number is 6 ones more than 772. What is the number?

   _____

 Writing and Reasoning How did you find the answer to Exercise 8?

_____

_____

_____

Value Clues

**Use the digits 8, 7, and 3 to make
a 3-digit number. Use all three digits.
Read the clues and write the number.**

1.

> **Clues:**
>
> The value of the digit 8
> in this number is 80.
>
> The value of the digit 7
> in this number is not 7.

The number is _____.

2.

> **Clues:**
>
> The value of the digit 8
> in this number is 800.
>
> The value of the digit 7
> in this number is not 70.

The number is _____.

3.

> **Clues:**
>
> The value of the digit 8
> in this number is 8.
>
> The value of the digit 7
> in this number is not 700.

The number is _____.

4.

> **Clues:**
>
> The value of the digit 7
> in this number is 70.
>
> The value of the digit 3
> in this number is not 300.

The number is _____.

 Writing and Reasoning Write a different 3-digit
number. Then write clues for your number.

_____

_____

Name _____

Say It Another Way

Write the number in two different ways.

1.

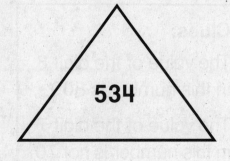

534

_____

_____

2.

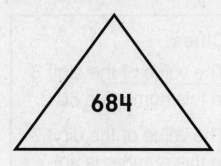

684

_____

_____

3.

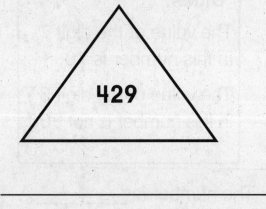

429

_____

_____

4.

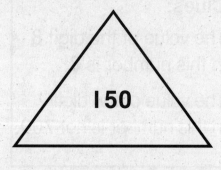

150

_____

_____

 Writing and Reasoning Look at Exercise 2.

What is a third way to write the number 684?

_____

_____

Cross-Number Puzzle

Use each clue to write a 3-digit number.
Put one digit in each square to complete the puzzle.

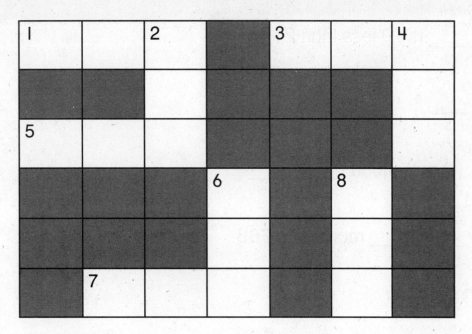

Across

1. 3 hundreds 6 tens 19 ones
3. 1 hundred 25 tens 1 one
5. 2 hundreds 4 tens 13 ones
7. 6 hundreds 7 tens 20 ones

Down

2. 8 hundreds 12 tens 3 ones
4. 17 tens 6 ones
6. 4 hundreds 2 tens 10 ones
8. 3 hundreds 12 tens 3 ones

Writing and Reasoning Choose one of the
puzzle clues. Write two other ways to show this number
using hundreds, tens, and ones.

_____

_____

Name _____

Missing Numbers

Write the missing number to make the sentence true.

1. _____ is 10 less than 214.

2. _____ is 100 less than 1,000.

3. 603 is 10 more than _____.

4. 888 is _____ more than 788.

Count on by 10s.

5. 950, _____, _____, _____, _____, _____

6. 782, _____, _____, _____, _____, _____

Count back by 10s.

7. 129, _____, _____, _____, _____, _____

8. 333, _____, _____, _____, _____, _____

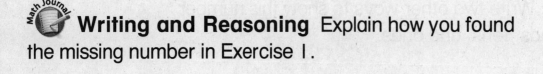 **Writing and Reasoning** Explain how you found
the missing number in Exercise 1.

_____

_____

Find the Number Pattern

Help the squirrel find a path to the tree. Connect acorns that show a pattern of counting on by 10s.

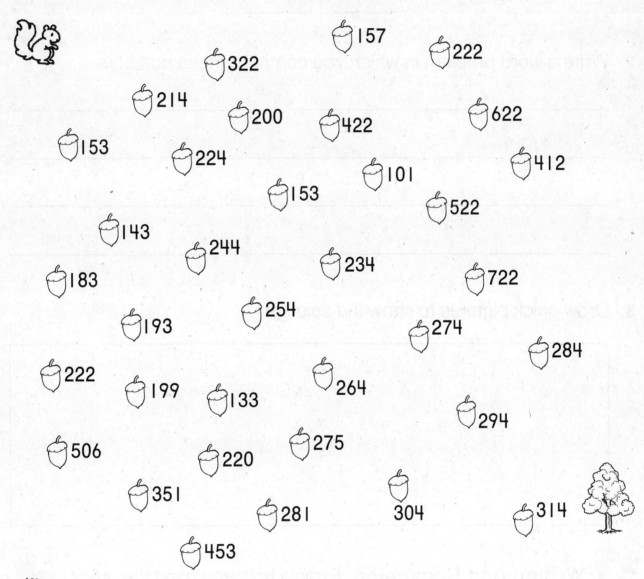

Writing and Reasoning Describe how you found the first few numbers in the pattern.

_____

_____

_____

Find the Greater Number

1. Use the digits 4, 2, 7, 3, 0, and 5 to write two
   3-digit numbers.

   _____ _____

2. Write a word problem in which you compare these numbers.

   _____

   _____

   _____

   _____

3. Draw quick pictures to show the solution.

Writing and Reasoning Explain how you used the quick
pictures to solve your problem.

_____

_____

Comparing

Write each digit once to make the comparison true.

1. 9, 6, 1

   ___ ___ ___ < 178

2. 2, 5, 8

   ___ ___ ___ < 852

3. 9, 3, 4

   ___ ___ ___ > 439

4. 1, 8, 7

   187 > ___ ___ ___

5. 2, 6

   42 ___ > 2 ___ 1

6. 7, 3

   33 ___ > ___ 36

7. 8, 5

   3 ___ 7 < ___ 67

8. 9, 5, 4

   ___ ___ 7 > ___ 67

 Writing and Reasoning Write a digit to make the comparison true.

___ 84 > 873

Is there more than one correct answer? Explain.

_____

_____

_____

Name _____

The Middle of the Train

Use the numbers in the clouds. Write each number in a train car. Use each number once. Check that the numbers for each train are in the correct order.

843   921   321   459

1.

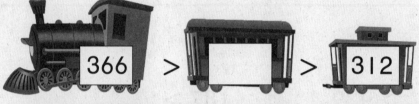

366 > [ ] > 312

2.

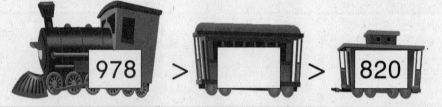

978 > [ ] > 820

3.

432 < [ ] < 465

4.

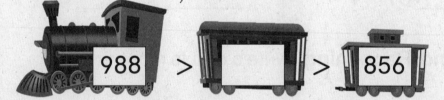

988 > [ ] > 856

Writing and Reasoning Complete. Explain your choice.

675 < _____ < 824

_____

_____

_____

Tic + Tac + Toe

**Write the sums in each box.
Draw a line through three boxes in a row
that have one of the same sums.**

9 + 0 = ___ 0 + 7 = ___	6 + 0 = ___ 0 + 8 = ___	5 + 0 = ___ 0 + 2 = ___
5 + 5 = ___ 5 + 4 = ___	4 + 4 = ___ 4 + 5 = ___	3 + 3 = ___ 3 + 4 = ___
7 + 4 = ___ 4 + 7 = ___	6 + 6 = ___ 6 + 5 = ___	6 + 3 = ___ 3 + 6 = ___

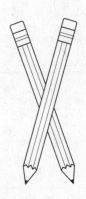

7 + 8 = ___ 8 + 7 = ___	9 + 2 = ___ 2 + 9 = ___	4 + 4 = ___ 4 + 3 = ___
9 + 9 = ___ 9 + 8 = ___	0 + 0 = ___ 4 + 0 = ___	5 + 2 = ___ 2 + 5 = ___
9 + 9 = ___ 9 + 10 = ___	6 + 6 = ___ 6 + 7 = ___	6 + 1 = ___ 1 + 6 = ___

Writing and Reasoning Draw a loop around
each box with number sentences that have 0 as an
addend. Did you win Tic + Tac + Toe again? Explain why.

_____

_____

Make-a-Ten Again

**Circle ten. Then write the make-a-ten fact
to solve for the total number of animals.**

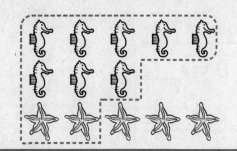

$$\frac{8}{10} + \frac{5}{3} = \frac{?}{13}$$

$$\underline{} + \underline{} = ?$$
$$\underline{} + \underline{} = \underline{}$$

$$\underline{} + \underline{} = ?$$
$$\underline{} + \underline{} = \underline{}$$

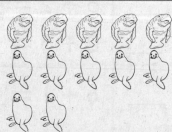

$$\underline{} + \underline{} = ?$$
$$\underline{} + \underline{} = \underline{}$$

Writing and Reasoning How did you decide
which make-a-ten fact to use? Explain.

_____

_____

Finding Sums

Use two sets of cards for numbers 0–10.
Play with a classmate.
Take three cards to get three addends.
Write the sum.

	1st Card	2nd Card	3rd Card	Sum
1.				
2.				
3.				
4.				
5.				

Writing and Reasoning Explain how you decided which two numbers to add first for one of your sums.

_____

_____

_____

Related Facts

**A sum and one addend are written in the triangle.
Write the other addend. Then write an addition fact
and a related subtraction fact for the numbers.**

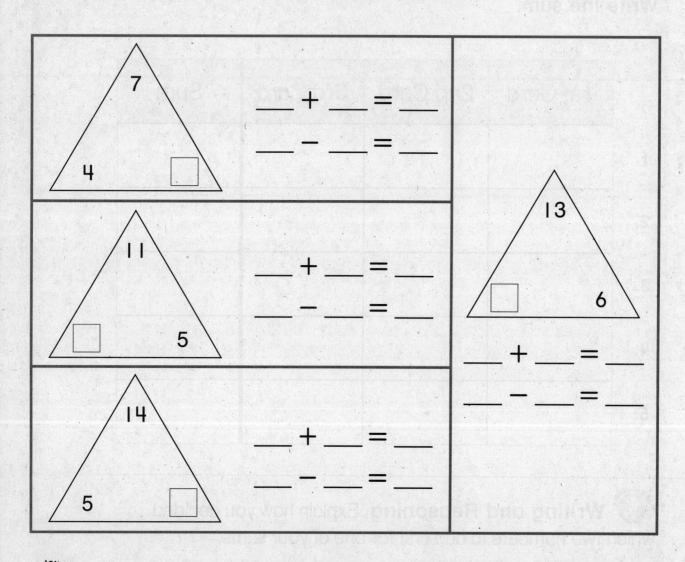

© Houghton Mifflin Harcourt School Publishers

Writing and Reasoning Draw
another triangle with a sum and one addend.
Have a partner write the missing addend
and the related addition and
subtraction facts.

Building Fact Families

Choose one number from each set of cards.
Write the numbers in the boxes.
Complete the fact family.
Use each number only once.

| 6 | 7 | 9 |

1. ☐ + ☐ = _____   _____ − _____ = _____

   ___ + ___ = _____   _____ − _____ = _____

2. ☐ + ☐ = _____   _____ − _____ = _____

   ___ + ___ = _____   _____ − _____ = _____

3. ☐ + ☐ = _____   _____ − _____ = _____

   ___ + ___ = _____   _____ − _____ = _____

Writing and Reasoning Explain how you know
which number sentences belong in the same fact family.

_____

_____

_____

Subtracting Across and Down

Each box has four subtraction sentences.

Two are written across. The other two are written down.

Fill in the missing numbers so that each subtraction sentence is correct.

1.

12	−	6	=	6
−				−
8				
=				=
4	−		=	1

2.

8	−	3	=	
−				−
=				=
4	−	4	=	

3.

	−	5	=	
−				−
				3
=				=
9	−		=	5

4.

	−	3	=	
−				−
6				4
=				=
	−	1	=	3

Writing and Reasoning How did you find the missing numbers in the top row in Exercise 4?

_____

_____

Picture It

Fill in the missing number.
Draw a picture and solve.

1. Alexia has 14 marbles. She gives _____ marbles to Sam. How many marbles does Alexia have left?

_____ marbles

2. Jennifer has 7 red marbles and _____ blue marbles. How many marbles does she have altogether?

_____ marbles

3. Carter had _____ marbles. He gave all the marbles to his brother. How many marbles does Carter have now?

_____ marbles

 Writing and Reasoning Explain how drawing a picture can help you solve a problem.

_____

_____

_____

What Is Missing?

Choose one number from the cards to complete the problem. Then write a number sentence to solve.

4	5	6
7	8	9

1. There are 10 red kites.
   There are _____ green kites.
   How many kites are there in all?

   ____ ◯ ____ ◯ ____

   _____ kites

2. Rachel has _____ blue shirts and 3 green shirts. How many shirts does she have in all?

   ____ ◯ ____ ◯ ____

   _____ shirts

3. Leslie has 13 coins.
   _____ coins are pennies.
   The rest are nickels.
   How many coins are nickels?

   ____ ◯ ____ ◯ ____

   _____ nickels

4. Grayson has 14 stamps.
   He gives _____ stamps to his sister. How many stamps does he have left?

   ____ ◯ ____ ◯ ____

   _____ stamps

Writing and Reasoning Explain how you know whether to add or subtract.

_____

_____

A Balancing Act

**Look at the numbers in each grid. Write numbers
in each row so that all four rows have the same sum.**

1.

2		2	
5	4	0	1
	3	2	
1	5		

2.

	3	4	
	2	1	
4			0
1	7	3	2

3.

5	4	3	2
6	2		
3		7	
1	2		5

4.

	6	4	
2			7
3	4	5	5
	8	3	

 Writing and Reasoning Explain how you
decided what numbers to write in the grid for Exercise 2.

_____

_____

_____

Name _____

Dominoes

Write the numbers for each domino.
Write = or ≠ to make the number sentence true.

1.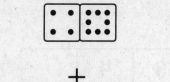

____ + ____   ◯   ____ + ____

2.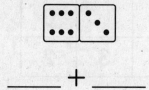

____ + ____   ◯   ____ + ____

3.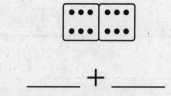

____ + ____   ◯   ____ + ____

Draw dots on the dominoes. Complete the number sentence.

4.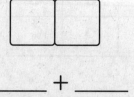

____ + ____   ◯   ____ + ____

 Writing and Reasoning Explain what
the = and ≠ signs mean.

_____

_____

_____

Break Apart to Match

Draw a line to connect each number sentence
on the left to its matching break-apart sentence
on the right. Then write the sum for each number
sentence to check your work.

17 + 4 = ____ •   • 50 + 1 = ____

27 + 6 = ____ •   • 20 + 7 = ____

45 + 6 = ____ •   • 60 + 7 = ____

32 + 9 = ____ •   • 20 + 1 = ____

18 + 9 = ____ •   • 40 + 4 = ____

66 + 7 = ____ •   • 40 + 1 = ____

39 + 5 = ____ •   • 30 + 3 = ____

58 + 9 = ____ •   • 70 + 3 = ____

 Writing and Reasoning Write a number
sentence to match with 50 + 6 = 56.

Match the Sums

Find each sum. Then draw a line to connect each number sentence on the left to the number sentence on the right that has the same sum.

$19 + 37 =$ _____ •   • $30 + 28 =$ _____

$43 + 18 =$ _____ •   • $20 + 36 =$ _____

$56 + 27 =$ _____ •   • $60 + 10 =$ _____

$32 + 19 =$ _____ •   • $31 + 20 =$ _____

$67 + 23 =$ _____ •   • $41 + 20 =$ _____

$29 + 29 =$ _____ •   • $40 + 44 =$ _____

$39 + 45 =$ _____ •   • $60 + 23 =$ _____

$58 + 12 =$ _____ •   • $70 + 20 =$ _____

Writing and Reasoning Write two pairs of addition sentences that have matching sums.

_____

_____

Name _____

Tens and Ones Combinations

Use the tens and ones numbers in the box to complete each problem. Some numbers can be used more than once. Then write the sums for the tens and for the ones.

50	4	30	9	20
40	7	60	8	
10	5	2	3	70

1. $\underline{\ \ 30\ \ }$ + _____
    + _____ + _____
    _____ + _____ = 92

2. _____ + _____
    + _____ + _____
    _____ + _____ = 71

3. _____ + _____
    + _____ + _____
    _____ + _____ = 93

4. _____ + _____
    + _____ + _____
    _____ + _____ = 100

 **Writing and Reasoning** Explain how you decided which tens and ones numbers to use for Exercise 4.

_____

Go Fish

Write the total number of tens and ones for each fish.

Write the sum on the tail. Use the code to color the fish.

52 → orange	61 → red	73 → green	84 → blue

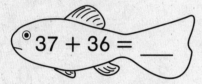

37 + 36 = ___

___ tens ___ones

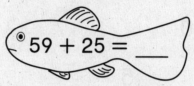

59 + 25 = ___

___ tens ___ones

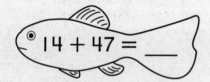

14 + 47 = ___

___ tens ___ones

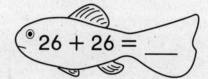

26 + 26 = ___

___ tens ___ones

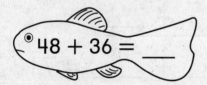

48 + 36 = ___

___ tens ___ones

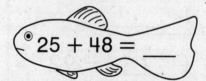

25 + 48 = ___

___ tens ___ones

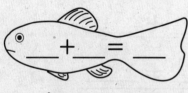

___ + ___ = ___

___ tens ___ones

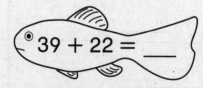

39 + 22 = ___

___ tens ___ones

Writing and Reasoning Write a number sentence for the blank fish so that there are two fish for each color listed.

What is the Problem?

**The models below can be used to solve problems.
Write a word problem for each model and solve it.
The first problem is started for you.**

1.

Tens	Ones

Jimmy collected 35 apples.

_____

_____

_____

_____

2.

Tens	Ones

_____

_____

_____

_____

_____

 Writing and Reasoning

Draw quick pictures of a model
for another problem and solve.

Name _____

Adding Errors

Find the errors in the addition problems.
Circle the errors. Then show how to solve
the problem correctly.

1.

Tens	Ones
(1)	
1	2
+ 4	9
(5)	1

Tens	Ones
[1]	
1	2
+ 4	9
6	1

2.

Tens	Ones
[1]	
3	7
+ 4	5
8	3

Tens	Ones
[ ]	
3	7
+ 4	5

3.

Tens	Ones
[2]	
2	6
+ 2	6
4	2

Tens	Ones
[ ]	
2	6
+ 2	6

4.

Tens	Ones
[1]	
7	2
+ 1	9
8	1

Tens	Ones
[ ]	
7	2
+ 1	9

Writing and Reasoning Describe the error you
found in Exercise 4.

_____

_____

_____

_____

Trace the Path

Trace your way around the treasure map.

Find each sum. Draw the path by following the sums from least to greatest.

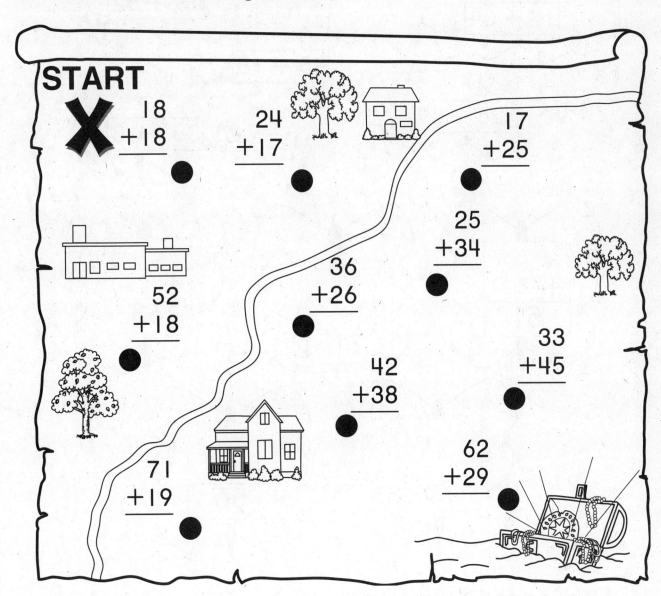

START

$$18 + 18$$

$$24 + 17$$

$$17 + 25$$

$$52 + 18$$

$$36 + 26$$

$$25 + 34$$

$$42 + 38$$

$$33 + 45$$

$$71 + 19$$

$$62 + 29$$

Writing and Reasoning What are two 2-digit numbers that have a sum of 83?

_____

Butterfly Addition

Match each problem on a caterpillar to the correct sum on a butterfly. You may wish to rewrite the problem on the butterfly.

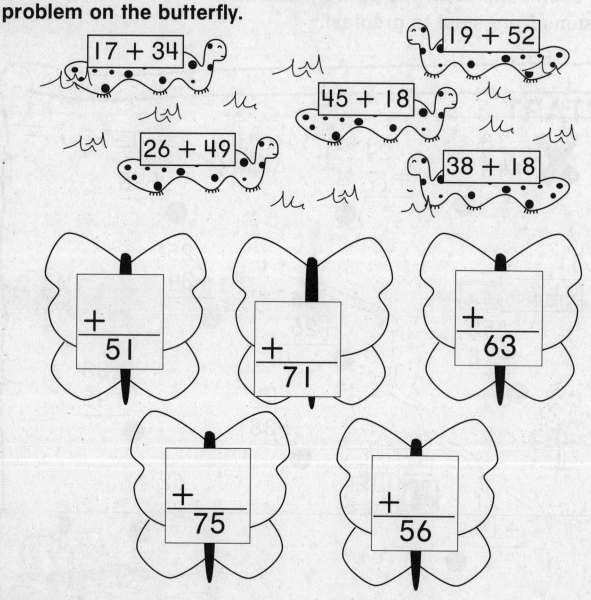

Writing and Reasoning Choose one of the sums. Write a number sentence that does not involve regrouping, using this sum and two 2-digit addends.

Balloon Addition

Solve.

1. There are 25 red balloons and 27 blue balloons. How many balloons are there in all?

   _____ balloons

2. There are 43 big balloons and 27 small balloons. How many balloons are there altogether?

   _____ balloons

3. Angel saw 17 balloons. Lisa saw 29 balloons. How many balloons did they see in all?

   _____ balloons

4. Andre and his dad flew 68 balloons altogether. Andre flew 37 balloons. How many balloons did Andre's dad fly?

   _____ balloons

 Writing and Reasoning Explain how you solved Exercise 4.

_____

_____

_____

Target Toss

Each child threw two bags at the target.
Estimate to answer the questions.

1. Sam's total score was less than 20 points. Which two numbers did Sam's bags land on?

13	18
20	5

2. Daniel's total score was greater than 50 points. Which two numbers did Daniel's bags land on?

30	23
10	16

3. Ali's total score was less than 50 points. Which two numbers did Ali's bags land on?

56	35
6	79

4. Emma's total score was greater than 100 points. Which two numbers did Emma's bags land on?

54	20
31	62

Writing and Reasoning Explain how you estimated to find the answer to Exercise 3.

_____

_____

_____

Name _____

Choose Three

Choose three numbers
for each exercise.
Write them in the
shapes. Write the sum.

⬤ 22	▢ 31	⬡ 17	▢ 43	⬡ 24
⬡ 45	⬤ 31	▢ 20	⬤ 38	⬡ 16

1. ▢
    ◯
  + ⬡
    _____

2. ▢
    ◯
  + ⬡
    _____

3. ▢
    ◯
  + ⬡
    _____

4. ▢
    ◯
  + ⬡
    _____

5. ▢
    ◯
  + ⬡
    _____

6. ▢
    ◯
  + ⬡
    _____

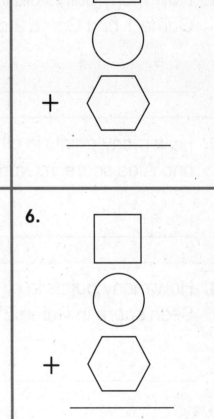

Writing and Reasoning Write an addition
sentence with three 2-digit addends that does not have
regrouping.

_____

Scoring Sums

The school basketball team played two games this week.

Use the charts to answer the questions. Write number sentences and solve.

Game 1	
Player	Points scored
Ray	18
Sean	12
Troy	9
Alec	15

Game 2	
Player	Points scored
Ray	25
Sean	13
Troy	21
Alec	20

1. How many points did Troy score in Game 1 and Game 2 altogether?

_____ _____ points

2. How many points in all did Ray and Alec score in Game 1?

_____ _____ points

3. How many points in all did Ray and Sean score in Game 2?

_____ _____ points

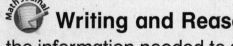 **Writing and Reasoning** Explain how you found the information needed to solve Exercise 3.

_____

_____

Name _____

A Maze of Thirties

**Help the kitten find the path to the ball of yarn.
Write the difference in each box. Color the boxes
that have a difference of 30, 31, or 32.**

$39 - 7 = $ ____	$34 - 9 = $ ____	$35 - 7 = $ ____
$41 - 9 = $ ____	$38 - 8 = $ ____	
$52 - 8 = $ ____	$38 - 7 = $ ____	
	$38 - 6 = $ ____	
$25 - 8 = $ ____	$40 - 8 = $ ____	$37 - 7 = $ ____
$27 - 6 = $ ____	$28 - 5 = $ ____	$39 - 8 = $ ____
		$37 - 6 = $ ____

Writing and Reasoning Write two number
sentences that each have a difference of 32 in the
empty boxes so the path goes on to the bowl of milk.

Subtraction Bingo

Find the difference for each subtraction problem.

Draw a line through spaces that have the same difference.

B I N G O

35 − 14 = ____	26 − 14 = ____	35 − 19 = ____	33 − 19 = ____	62 − 36 = ____
29 − 12 = ____	39 − 18 = ____	42 − 19 = ____	64 − 29 = ____	53 − 28 = ____
55 − 16 = ____	43 − 28 = ____	**Free Space**	32 − 19 = ____	53 − 12 = ____
52 − 9 = ____	61 − 25 = ____	41 − 13 = ____	47 − 26 = ____	68 − 39 = ____
57 − 19 = ____	62 − 17 = ____	46 − 28 = ____	54 − 17 = ____	40 − 19 = ____

Writing and Reasoning Write two subtraction problems that each have a difference of 28.

_____

_____

Choose the Numbers

Use the numbers below to make subtraction
problems with regrouping. Then solve. You
may wish to draw quick pictures for the problems.

28	33	45	57	39	36

Subtract _____ from _____.

_____ tens _____ ones

_____

Subtract _____ from _____.

_____ tens _____ ones

_____

Subtract _____ from _____.

_____ tens _____ ones

_____

Subtract _____ from _____.

_____ tens _____ ones

_____

Writing and Reasoning Which of the numbers above
could be subtracted from 84 without regrouping? Explain.

_____

_____

_____

The Lost Digits

These subtraction problems are missing some digits.

Can you put them back where they belong? Write the correct digits in the boxes.

1.

Tens	Ones
4	8
− 1	☐
3	4

2.

Tens	Ones
2	15
3̸	5̸
− 1	☐
1	6

3.

Tens	Ones
7	8
− ☐	6
2	2

1, 3, 4, 9, 5, 2, 8

4.

Tens	Ones
☐	18
4̸	8̸
− ☐	9
2	9

5.

Tens	Ones
4	☐
− 1	1
3	1

6.

Tens	Ones
2	8
− 1	☐
1	0

 Writing and Reasoning How did you choose which digit to use in Exercise 6?

_____

_____

Name _____

Race to Zero

Each car has a number. Subtract that number from each stop along the road until there is a difference of zero.

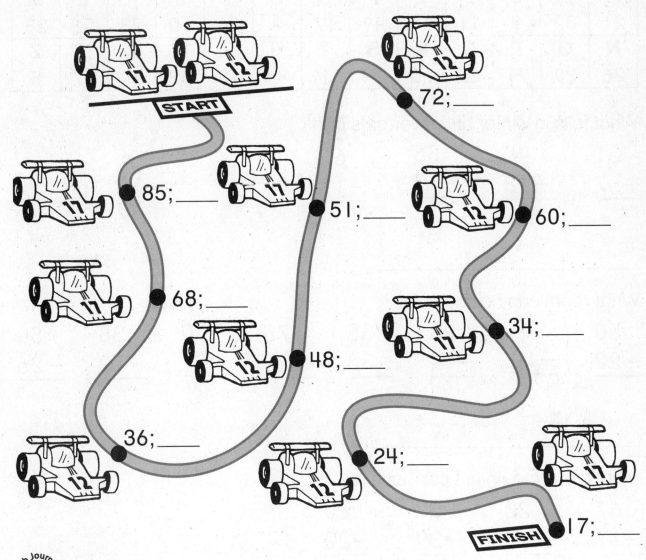

Writing and Reasoning Write a subtraction sentence that has a difference of 17 and a subtraction sentence that has a difference of 12.

_____

_____

Subtraction Riddles

Solve each subtraction problem. Each difference
matches with a letter. Write those letters below
the differences to solve each riddle.

A	B	C	D	E	F	G	H	I	J	K	L	M
21	32	9	11	40	49	17	2	16	10	23	51	28

N	O	P	Q	R	S	T	U	V	W	X	Y	Z
26	29	71	65	50	14	1	34	18	52	44	47	8

What falls in winter but never gets hurt?

$$\begin{array}{r} 21 \\ -\ 7 \\ \hline \end{array} \qquad \begin{array}{r} 44 \\ -18 \\ \hline \end{array} \qquad \begin{array}{r} 38 \\ -\ 9 \\ \hline \end{array} \qquad \begin{array}{r} 63 \\ -11 \\ \hline \end{array}$$

_____

What room can no one enter?

$$\begin{array}{r} 50 \\ -22 \\ \hline \end{array} \quad \begin{array}{r} 44 \\ -10 \\ \hline \end{array} \quad \begin{array}{r} 28 \\ -14 \\ \hline \end{array} \quad \begin{array}{r} 38 \\ -36 \\ \hline \end{array} \quad \begin{array}{r} 75 \\ -25 \\ \hline \end{array} \quad \begin{array}{r} 50 \\ -21 \\ \hline \end{array} \quad \begin{array}{r} 38 \\ -\ 9 \\ \hline \end{array} \quad \begin{array}{r} 54 \\ -26 \\ \hline \end{array}$$

_____

What has a mouth but can never eat?

$$\begin{array}{r} 67 \\ -17 \\ \hline \end{array} \qquad \begin{array}{r} 28 \\ -12 \\ \hline \end{array} \qquad \begin{array}{r} 57 \\ -39 \\ \hline \end{array} \qquad \begin{array}{r} 60 \\ -20 \\ \hline \end{array} \qquad \begin{array}{r} 59 \\ -\ 9 \\ \hline \end{array}$$

_____

Writing and Reasoning Write two subtraction
problems that each have a difference matching with **N**.

Name _____

How Many Could There Be?

Write and solve two subtraction problems that show how many of each animal there might be. Then write the numbers.

1. There are four different kinds of animals on the farm.

   There is a different number of each kind of animal.

   There are 19 more cows than sheep.

   There are 19 more ducks than hens.

   There are more hens than cows.

   _____ cows

   _____ sheep

   _____ ducks

   _____ hens

 Writing and Reasoning How did you find the answers?

_____

_____

_____

Name _____

The Art of Differences

Draw to show each problem. Then solve.

Emilio needs 34 markers for his project. He has only 22 markers. How many more markers does he need? _____ more markers	37 projects were on the counter. 24 students picked up their projects. How many projects are still on the counter? _____ projects
Terrell had 70 pieces of paper. He used 36 pieces of paper for drawings. How many pieces of paper does he have left? _____ pieces of paper	26 students made paintings in class. 17 of those students are girls. How many of those students are boys? _____ boys

 Writing and Reasoning Write your own subtraction word problem about art class.

_____

_____

_____

Find the Numbers

The answer for each problem is given. You will need to choose numbers from the box to complete each problem.

17	45	48	54	61	63

1. Alex had _____ points in the spelling game. Sophie had

   _____ points in the spelling game. How many more points did Sophie have in the game than Alex?   __15__ more points

   _____

2. Tim has a box of sports cards.

   He took _____ cards out of the box and _____ cards were left in the box.

   How many cards were in the box to start with?   __62__ cards

   _____

 Writing and Reasoning Describe how you chose the numbers for Exercise 2.

   _____

   _____

   _____

From 100 to 25

Look at the number given. First, subtract that number from 100. Then, find a number to subtract from that difference to get to 25. The first problem is started for you.

1. 37	$\begin{array}{r} 100 \\ - \ 37 \\ \hline 63 \end{array}$	$\begin{array}{r} 63 \\ - \ \_\_\_ \\ \hline 25 \end{array}$
2. 52		
3. 14		

Writing and Reasoning Explain how you found the number to subtract to get to 25 in the second step.

_____

_____

_____

Survey Time

Margo asked 18 classmates about their favorite
animals. Use the clues to complete the chart.

Favorite Animal	
Animal	**Tally**
zebra	
giraffe	
elephant	IIII I

1. One more classmate voted for zebra than for
   elephant. Draw tally marks for zebra.

   _____

2. The other classmates voted for giraffe.
   How many tally marks should Margo draw
   for giraffe?

   _____ tally marks

   _____

3. Draw tally marks for giraffe.

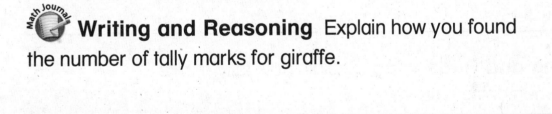 **Writing and Reasoning** Explain how you found
the number of tally marks for giraffe.

_____

_____

_____

Tally Time

Jack asked 20 classmates to vote for their favorite summer activity.

- Six classmates voted for swimming.
- Four more classmates voted for hiking than for swimming.
- The other classmates voted for biking.

1. Complete the tally chart to show how the classmates voted.

Favorite Summer Activity		
Activity	Tally	Total

2. List the activities in order from the activity that the most classmates chose to the activity that the fewest classmates chose.

_____

Writing and Reasoning Explain how tally marks are helpful when doing a survey.

_____

_____

Lots of Pets

Lily took a survey of her classmates to find their
favorite pet.

- Eight classmates voted for cat.

- Four fewer classmates voted for dog than cat.

- Eight classmates voted for fish.

1. Use the clues above to complete the tally chart and the
pictograph for Lily's survey.

Favorite Pet	
Pet	**Tally**
cat	
dog	
fish	

Favorite Pet					
cat					
dog					
fish					

Key: Each ☺ stands for 2 children.

2. How many classmates in all voted in the survey?

_____ classmates

Writing and Reasoning Describe how the
numbers of pictures in the pictograph would be different
if each picture stood for 4 children.

_____

_____

_____

Lots of Squares

Nina drew some squares.
She wrote letters in the squares.

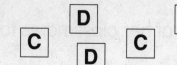 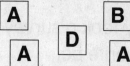

1. Draw bars to show the
   number of each kind
   of square Nina drew.

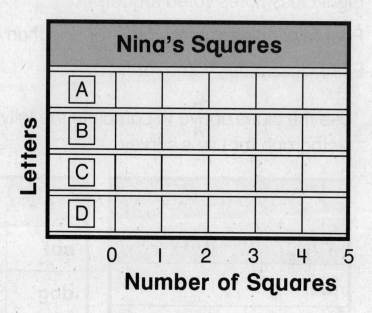

Nina's Squares

Letters
A
B
C
D

0 1 2 3 4 5
Number of Squares

2. Write a question you can answer by using the data in
   the graph. Ask a classmate to answer your question.

_____

_____

_____

Writing and Reasoning How did you know how
long to draw the bars for each kind of square?

_____

_____

_____

Asking Questions

Jeremy made a bar graph to show his classmates' favorite kind of music.

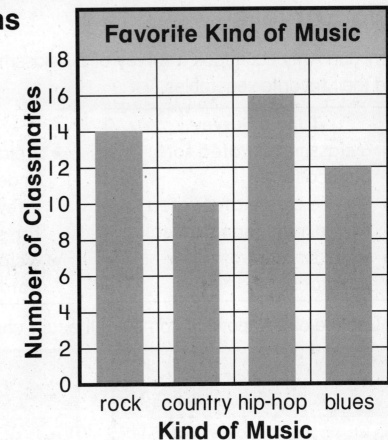

Number of Classmates

18
16
14
12
10
8
6
4
2
0

Favorite Kind of Music

rock   country   hip-hop   blues
Kind of Music

Write a question about the graph for each answer.

1. _____

   _____ Answer: Country

2. _____

   _____ Answer: 2 more votes

Writing and Reasoning What is the scale on the graph? Explain what the scale tells you.

_____

_____

Two Surveys

Tami and Amy each took a survey of 20 classmates to find their favorite vegetables.

Tami's Survey
• 6 classmates voted for broccoli.
• 3 more classmates voted for carrots than broccoli.
• 5 classmates voted for potatoes.

Amy's Survey
• 7 classmates voted for broccoli.
• 2 fewer classmates voted for carrots than broccoli.
• 8 classmates voted for potatoes.

1. Use the clues above to complete the tally charts.

Tami's Survey Favorite Vegetable	
Vegetable	Tally
broccoli	
carrots	
potatoes	

Amy's Survey Favorite Vegetable	
Vegetable	Tally
broccoli	
carrots	
potatoes	

2. Which vegetable did the most classmates choose in each survey?

Tami's survey: _____   Amy's survey: _____

Writing and Reasoning Explain how you knew how many tally marks to draw for carrots in Tami's chart.

_____

_____

Domino Break

Each set of dominoes shows a 3-digit addend on top and another on the bottom. Break apart the addends. Solve and write the sum.

1.

$600 + 40 + 3$
$100 + 10 + 2$
755

2.

___ + ___ + __
___ + ___ + __
___

3.

___ + ___ + __
___ + ___ + __
___

4.

___ + ___ + __
___ + ___ + __
___

5.

___ + ___ + __
___ + ___ + __
___

6.

___ + ___ + __
___ + ___ + __
___

Writing and Reasoning Draw your own set of dominoes to show 3-digit addition. Give it to a classmate to solve.

3-Digit Scramble

Use the digits to make two addends for a problem
in which you regroup the ones. Solve.

1. 6, 5, 3, 1, 2, 4

Hundreds	Tens	Ones
+		

2. 4, 4, 1, 3, 3, 9

Hundreds	Tens	Ones
+		

3. 2, 1, 3, 7, 2, 4

Hundreds	Tens	Ones
+		

4. 4, 3, 2, 2, 1, 6

Hundreds	Tens	Ones
+		

 Writing and Reasoning How did you make sure
the ones would need to be regrouped?

_____

_____

_____

Name _____

Triple Digits

Use the numbers on the shirts to make an addition problem. Write the sum.

1.

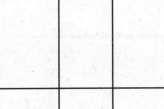

2.

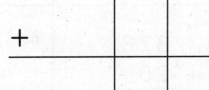

3.

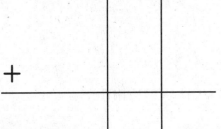

4.

Writing and Reasoning Write your own 3-digit addition problem with regrouping in the tens. Give it to a classmate to solve.

Name _____

Paint by Regrouping

Find each sum. Use blue to circle the problems in which you regrouped twice. Use green to circle the problems in which you regrouped once. Use yellow to circle the problems with no regrouping.

1. 127 + 293	2. 785 + 152	3. 825 + 123
4. 378 + 204	5. 561 + 327	6. 486 + 335
7. 237 + 522	8. 287 + 536	9. 709 + 216

 Writing and Reasoning Why do you sometimes need to regroup in 3-digit addition?

_____

_____

_____

Addition Wheels

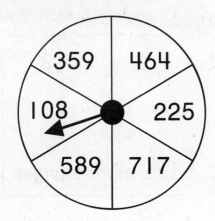 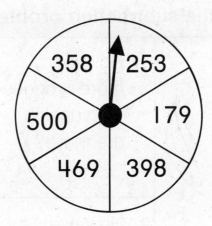

Nia wants to find two addends that have a sum of 717. She spins the pointer on each addition wheel. On which two numbers does Nia need the pointers to stop to have a sum of 717?

_____ and _____

What are two other numbers on which the pointers could stop that have a sum of 717?

_____ and _____

Writing and Reasoning Write and solve two addition problems using numbers from the spinners.

_____

_____

What is the Difference?

Use the information on the farmer's list to
write and solve the subtraction problem.

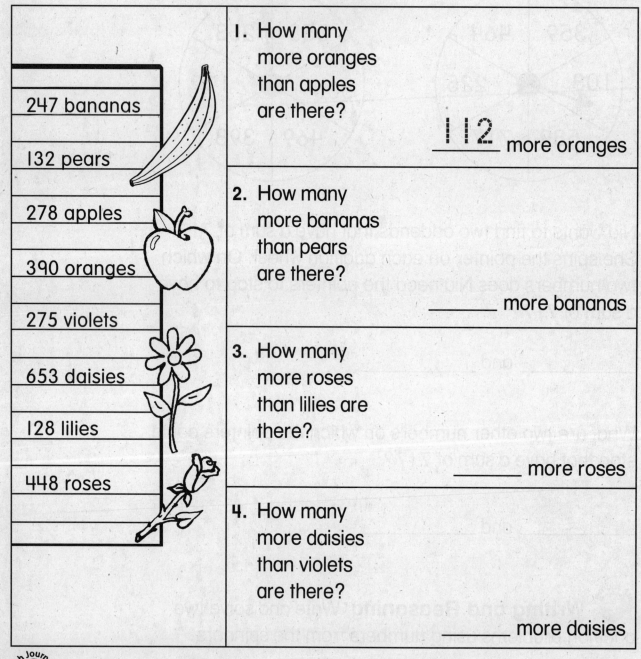

247 bananas

132 pears

278 apples

390 oranges

275 violets

653 daisies

128 lilies

448 roses

1. How many
   more oranges
   than apples
   are there?

   __112__ more oranges

2. How many
   more bananas
   than pears
   are there?

   _____ more bananas

3. How many
   more roses
   than lilies are
   there?

   _____ more roses

4. How many
   more daisies
   than violets
   are there?

   _____ more daisies

Writing and Reasoning Use the list to write your
own subtraction problem. Have a classmate solve it.

Name _____

Subtraction Steps

Solve each subtraction problem on the ladder to reach the top.

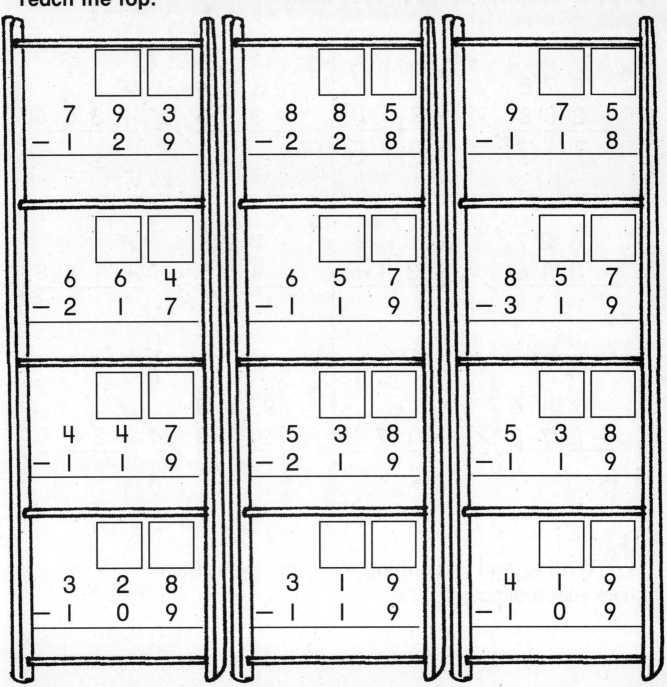

 Writing and Reasoning Write a 3-digit subtraction problem of your own that has no regrouping.

Name _____

Check It Out

Solve the subtraction problem. Then complete the addition problem to check your work.

1.
$$
\begin{array}{r} \overset{6}{\cancel{9}}\;\overset{15}{\cancel{7}}\,5 \\ -\;2\;5\;8 \\ \hline 7\;1\;7 \end{array}
\qquad
\begin{array}{r} \overset{1}{7}\;1\;7 \\ +\;2\;5\;8 \\ \hline 9\;7\;5 \end{array}
$$

2.
$$
\begin{array}{r} 8\;4\;9 \\ -\;3\;5\;5 \\ \hline \end{array}
\qquad
\begin{array}{r} \\ +\;3\;5\;5 \\ \hline \end{array}
$$

3.
$$
\begin{array}{r} 6\;2\;7 \\ -\;3\;4\;6 \\ \hline \end{array}
\qquad
\begin{array}{r} \\ +\;3\;4\;6 \\ \hline \end{array}
$$

4.
$$
\begin{array}{r} 7\;9\;8 \\ -\;4\;6\;8 \\ \hline \end{array}
\qquad
\begin{array}{r} \\ +\;4\;6\;8 \\ \hline \end{array}
$$

5.
$$
\begin{array}{r} 5\;4\;6 \\ -\;1\;7\;3 \\ \hline \end{array}
\qquad
\begin{array}{r} \\ +\;1\;7\;3 \\ \hline \end{array}
$$

6.
$$
\begin{array}{r} 4\;3\;8 \\ -\;2\;7\;0 \\ \hline \end{array}
\qquad
\begin{array}{r} \\ +\;2\;7\;0 \\ \hline \end{array}
$$

Writing and Reasoning Why does the addition check your subtraction?

_____

_____

_____

Name _____

More About Skip Counting

Rosa is skip counting by different numbers.
She starts counting at 0. Read the clues.
Circle the number she could be counting by.

1. Rosa shades 68, 70, and 72 on the hundred chart. She could be counting by:

   twos   fours   fives

1	2	3	4	5	6	7	8	9	10
11	12	13	14	15	16	17	18	19	20
21	22	23	24	25	26	27	28	29	30
31	32	33	34	35	36	37	38	39	40
41	42	43	44	45	46	47	48	49	50
51	52	53	54	55	56	57	58	59	60
61	62	63	64	65	66	67	68	69	70
71	72	73	74	75	76	77	78	79	80
81	82	83	84	85	86	87	88	89	90
91	92	93	94	95	96	97	98	99	100

2. Rosa shades 60 and 70 on the hundred chart. She could be counting by:

   threes   fours   fives

3. Rosa shades 39 on the hundred chart. She could be counting by:

   twos   threes   tens

4. Rosa shades 8 and 12 on the hundred chart. She could be counting by:

   threes   fours   fives

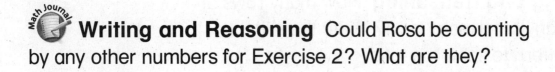 **Writing and Reasoning** Could Rosa be counting by any other numbers for Exercise 2? What are they?

_____

Sorting Stickers

Jamal's stickers need to be organized. Each type
of sticker must be grouped together. Different
types of stickers cannot be on the same page.
Each page can fit 2 rows of 3 stickers.

Draw a diagram to show the pages.

1. How many pages
   do you need for ♡?

   _____

2. How many pages
   do you need for ☺?

   _____

3. How many pages
   do you need for ☆?

   _____

4. How many pages
   do you need for ☾?

   _____

Writing and Reasoning How many rows of
3 stickers can Jamal make in all? Write the skip
counting pattern to show the total.

_____

_____

Name _____

Tell a Story

Complete the table to show a pattern.
Tell a story about the pattern.

1.

number of _____	1				
number of _____	5				

_____

_____

2.

number of _____		2			
number of _____		8			

_____

_____

Writing and Reasoning Write a problem to go with the first table.

_____

_____

_____

Same Total, Different Groups

- Write two ways to add equal groups to get the number of objects.
- Draw a picture for one of the ways.
- Complete the multiplication sentence.

1. There are 16 chairs.

____ + ____ = 16

____ + ____ + ____ + ____ = 16

____ × ____ = 16

2. There are 12 cars.

____ + ____ = 12

____ + ____ + ____ = 12

____ × ____ = 12

3. There are 8 apples.

____ + ____ = 8

____ + ____ + ____ + ____ = 8

____ × ____ = 8

Writing and Reasoning For Exercise 2, what is another way to add equal groups to get 12 cars?

_____

Name _____

Make Equal Rows

Fill in the blank in each problem with one of these numbers: 2, 3, 4, 5, or 6. Shade squares to model the problem. Write the multiplication sentence.

1. There are 5 rows of desks.

   _____ desks are in each row.
   How many desks are there in all?

   _____ desks

   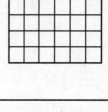

   _____

2. There are _____ rows of cars.
   4 cars are in each row.
   How many cars are there in all?

   _____ cars

   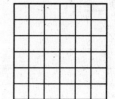

   _____

3. There are 3 shelves of books.

   _____ books are on each shelf.
   How many books are there in all?

   _____ books

   _____

Writing and Reasoning Explain how you knew
how many squares to shade for Exercise 1.

_____

_____

_____

Find the Mistakes

**All of the number sentences below show
multiplying with 2. Some of the multiplication
sentences have the wrong answer. Circle them.
Then write the multiplication sentence correctly.**

You may wish to use pairs of stars to skip count.

1. $7 \times 2 = 14$

_____

2. $6 \times 2 = 8$

_____

3. $5 \times 2 = 7$

_____

4. $3 \times 2 = 6$

_____

5. $4 \times 2 = 6$

_____

6. $8 \times 2 = 10$

_____

7. $2 \times 2 = 4$

_____

8. $9 \times 2 = 11$

_____

 Writing and Reasoning Look at all the
multiplication sentences that had wrong answers.
What was the mistake?

_____

_____

Missing Numbers

**Find the missing number in each multiplication
sentence. Draw a picture to check your answer.**

1. $5 \times 5 =$ _____

2. _____ $\times 5 = 10$

3. _____ $\times 5 = 15$

4. $4 \times$ _____ $= 20$

5. $6 \times 5 =$ _____

6. $8 \times$ _____ $= 40$

Writing and Reasoning Write your own
multiplication sentence that has a missing number.
Have a partner find the missing number.

_____

Compared to Me

Have a classmate cut a piece of string to match your height. Compare the length of the string to each real object. Check the correct box with an X.

	Find the object.	Shorter than the string	Longer than the string
1.			
2.			
3.			
4.			

Writing and Reasoning Find something else longer than your piece of string. Write a sentence to describe what you found.

_____

_____

_____

Compare to Measure

1. Lisa's paintbrush is about 8 buttons long. A piece of chalk is about 4 buttons long. About how many pieces of chalk long is the paintbrush?

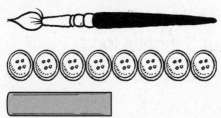

about _____ pieces of chalk

2. The frame is 2 pencils long. A pencil is about 3 erasers long. About how many erasers long is the frame?

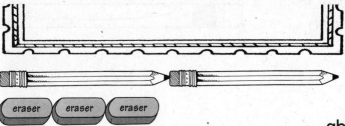

about _____ erasers

3. A party sandwich is 4 marker boxes long. Each box of markers is 2 stickers long. About how many stickers long is the sandwich?

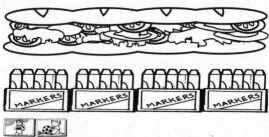

about _____ stickers

Writing and Reasoning If an eraser in Exercise 2 is 2 buttons long, about how many erasers long is the paintbrush in Exercise 1?

The Long and Short of It

Use each picture to estimate the length of a classroom object. Draw and label the object below the picture.

1. The string is about 2 inches long.
   Find an object that is about 3 inches long.

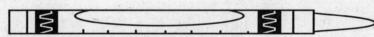

2. The crayon is about 4 inches long.
   Find an object that is
   about 7 inches long.

3. The paperclip is about 1 inch long.
   Find an object that is about 5 inches long.

 Writing and Reasoning How did you use the pictures to estimate?

_____

_____

Measure the Tools

Measure all Carpenter Dan's tools with your ruler.
Below each tool, write about how long it is.
Circle the tools that are shorter than 5 inches.

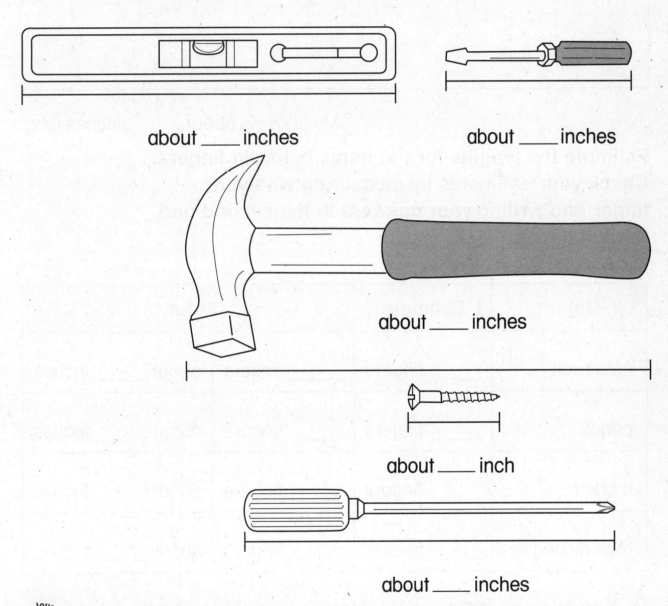

about ____ inches   about ____ inches

about ____ inches

about ____ inch

about ____ inches

Writing and Reasoning Draw another tool that Carpenter Dan might have with him. Measure it and write the length.

Handy Measuring

Trace the outline of your index finger. Measure your finger outline with an inch ruler and write down about how many inches long it is.

My finger is about _____ inches long.

Estimate the lengths for the items below in fingers. Check your estimates by measuring with your finger and writing your answers in the second and third columns.

Object	Estimate	Actual	
notebook	_____ fingers	_____ fingers	about _____ inches
pencil	_____ fingers	_____ fingers	about _____ inches
marker	_____ fingers	_____ fingers	about _____ inches
tape dispenser	_____ fingers	_____ fingers	about _____ inches

Writing and Reasoning Why would it be useful to be able to estimate measurements using your finger?

_____

_____

Map Measurements

Using a ruler, measure from point to point on the map.

Write each distance to the nearest inch.

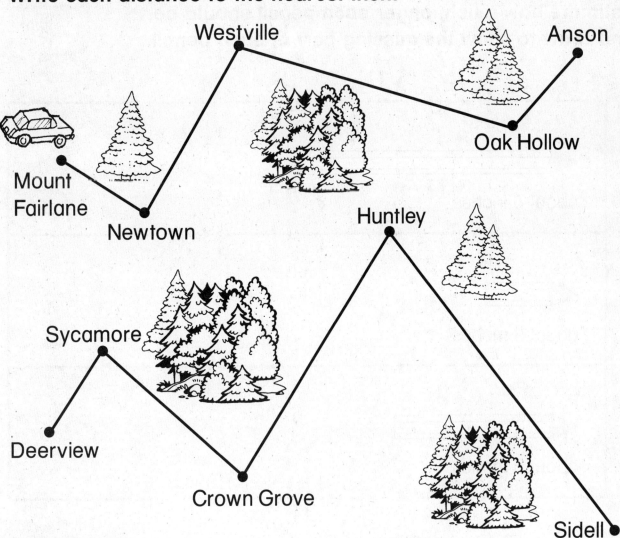

Math Journal **Writing and Reasoning** Find the distance from Mount Fairlane to Anson. Then find the distance from Deerview to Sidell. Which is greater? Explain.

_____

_____

_____

Name _____

Make Pencils

**Only part of each pencil is shown.
Look at the measurement below each pencil
to see how long that pencil needs to be.
Estimate how much longer each pencil should be,
and draw to show the missing part of each pencil.**

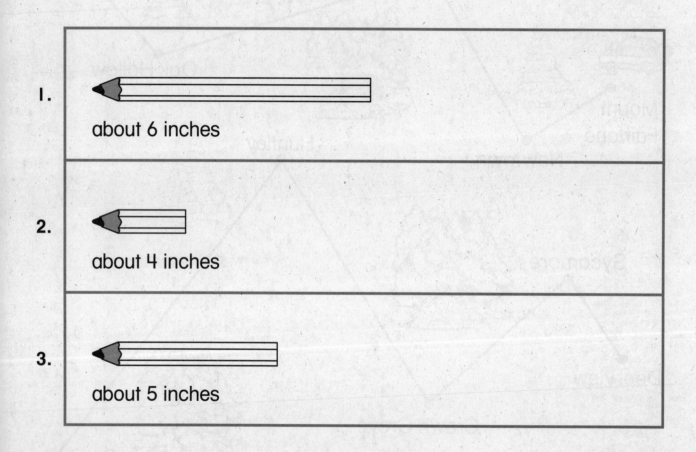

1. about 6 inches

2. about 4 inches

3. about 5 inches

Writing and Reasoning Measure each
pencil with an inch ruler. Were your estimates
close to the actual measurements? Explain.

_____

_____

_____

How Tall Are You?

Work with a partner. Lie on the floor and ask your partner to place a piece of tape on the floor at the top of your head and at the bottom of your feet.

Measure to find your height to the nearest inch. Then measure to find your height to the nearest foot.

Write your measurements below.

I am _____ inches tall.

I am about _____ feet tall.

Writing and Reasoning Twenty-seven inches is the same as 2 feet 3 inches. What is your height in feet and inches?

Length Riddles

Find a real object to fit the clues.

Measure the object. Remember to label your measurement with the unit you used (inches, feet, yards).

Then draw and label the object.

	Find an object.	Measure it.	Draw and label it.
1.	I am longer than 6 inches but shorter than 1 foot.	___ ___	_____
2.	I am longer than 1 foot but shorter than 1 yard.	___ ___	_____
3.	I am longer than 1 yard.	___ ___	_____

Writing and Reasoning Write a riddle for a classmate to solve. Have your classmate find an object, measure it, and draw it.

Centimeter Clips

Read each problem. Write your measurement.

Use small paper clips to measure. Each small paper clip is about 3 centimeters long.

1. This is part of a toy train track.

   About how many centimeters long is it?

   about _____ centimeters

2. This caboose is from John's collection.

   About how many centimeters long is it?

   about _____ centimeters

3. John needs to buy an engine for his train.

   About how many centimeters long is it?

   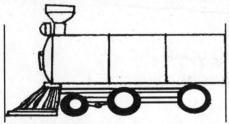

   about _____ centimeters

Writing and Reasoning Suppose an object in your classroom is about 5 small paper clips long. About how many centimeters long is it?

Colorful Vegetables

Color the vegetables that are 10 centimeters or longer yellow.

Color the vegetables that are shorter than 10 centimeters green.

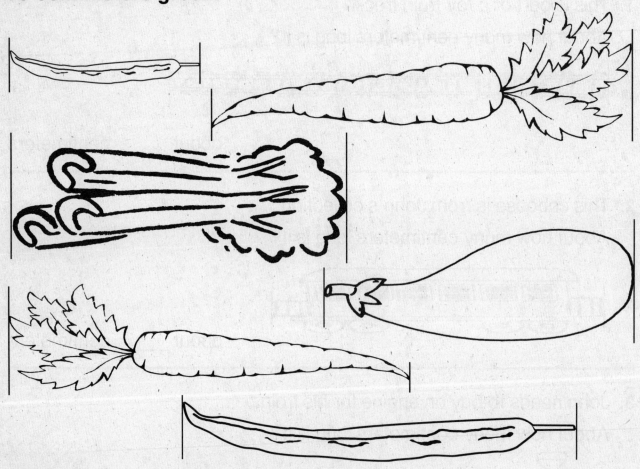

Writing and Reasoning If you lined up all the same-color vegetables end to end in two different rows, which row would be longer? Explain.

_____

_____

_____

Name _____

Measure by Hand

Make an estimate. Then measure real objects.

1. Use your  to measure.

   | Estimate: _____ fingers |

   | Actual: _____ fingers |

2. Use your 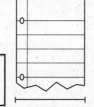 to measure.

   | Estimate: _____ palms |

   | Actual: _____ palms |

3. Use your 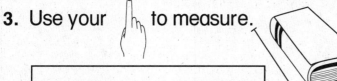 to measure.

   | Estimate: _____ fingers |

   | Actual: _____ fingers |

 Writing and Reasoning In Exercises 1–3, you
used different parts of your hand as measurement units.
Which unit was the best unit to use? Explain.

_____

_____

_____

Meters and Centimeters

Find real objects that fit the clues.
Measure each object. Use *centimeters* or
meters for the units. Then draw and label it.

	Find an object.	Measure it.	Draw and label it.
1.	I am shorter than 10 centimeters.	_____ _____	_____
2.	I am longer than 50 centimeters but shorter than 1 meter.	_____ _____	_____
3.	I am longer than 1 meter.	_____ _____	_____

Writing and Reasoning How much longer is
the object in Exercise 2 than the object in Exercise 1?
Explain.

Name _____

Measurement Hike

Help Benino and Rory take a few measurements on their hike. Draw to connect an item to what you would use to measure it. You may use more than one tool to measure an item or use a tool more than once. Be sure to use every tool at least once.

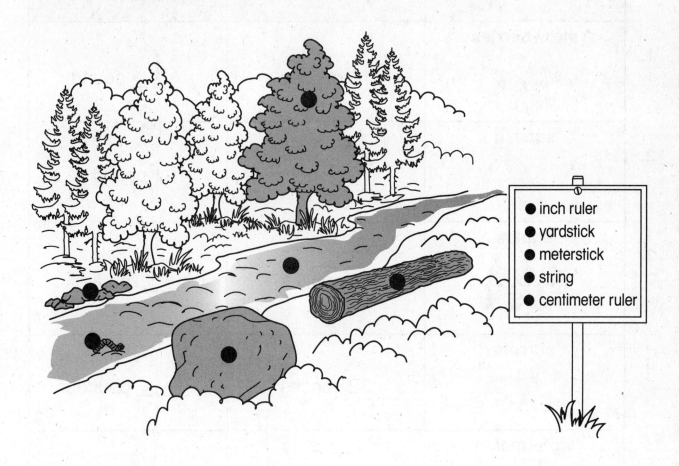

- inch ruler
- yardstick
- meterstick
- string
- centimeter ruler

Writing and Reasoning How did you decide which tools to match to the items being measured?

_____

_____

Grocery Shopping

Celenia goes grocery shopping with her father.
Help Celenia find the weight of each item
in ounces and in pounds.

	Item	Weight in Ounces	Weight in Pounds
1.	strawberries	16 ounces	_____ pound
2.	squash	_____ ounces	1 pound
3.	apples	48 ounces	_____ pounds
4.	carrots	32 ounces	_____ pounds
5.	watermelon	_____ ounces	5 pounds

Writing and Reasoning Describe how you
found the answer for Exercise 5.

_____

_____

Measuring Mass

Look around the classroom.

Choose two objects to measure in grams.

Choose two objects to measure in kilograms.

Draw and write the name of each object.

Then measure.

Grams	Kilograms
Object 1 _____ mass: about _____ grams	**Object 1** _____ mass: about _____ kilograms
Object 2 _____ mass: about _____ grams	**Object 2** _____ mass: about _____ kilograms

Writing and Reasoning How did you decide whether to measure an object in grams or in kilograms?

_____

_____

What Is the Capacity?

1. Blake has a new fishbowl. The bowl holds 2 quarts of water. Blake has a 1-cup measure. How many cups of water will he need to fill the bowl?

_____ cups

2. Abby has 3 quarts of apple juice. How many cups can she fill with apple juice? Draw the cups.

_____ cups

3. Mr. Tees made 16 cups of applesauce. He wants to store the sauce in quart jars. How many jars will he need?

_____ quart jars

 Writing and Reasoning Explain how you solved Exercise 3.

_____

_____

_____

_____

Liter Beakers

Write the correct measurement for each mark on the liter beakers.

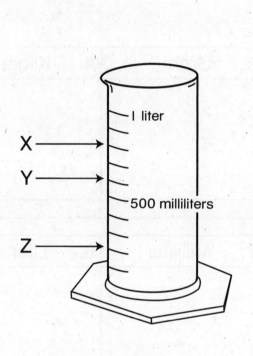

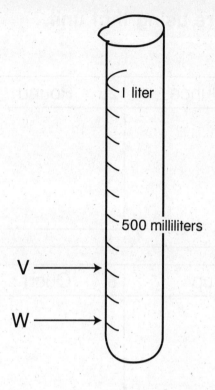

X _____ milliliters

Y _____ milliliters

Z _____ milliliters

V _____ milliliters

W _____ milliliters

Writing and Reasoning If each beaker is filled to the 1-liter line, how many milliliters will the two beakers hold altogether? How many liters?

_____   _____

Big or Small?

Look at the units of measure for weight, mass and capacity. Draw and label an object that you would measure using that unit.

1. Ounce	2. Pound	3. Gram	4. Kilogram

5. Cup	6. Quart	7. Milliliter	8. Liter

Writing and Reasoning Explain how you decide which unit of measure to use to measure weight, mass, and capacity.

_____

_____

_____

Name _____

Measure It

Draw and label three objects or containers
you can measure with each tool.

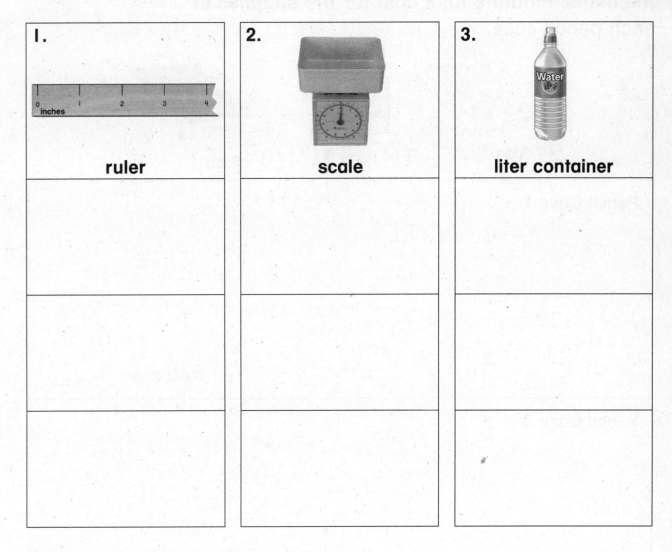

1.	2.	3.
ruler	scale	liter container

Writing and Reasoning Describe what you
are measuring when you use these tools.

ruler: _____

scale: _____

liter container: _____

Find the Total Cost

Draw a set of supplies for each pencil case. Each
case should have at least 3 items. Draw coins for
the items. Find the total cost for the supplies in
each pencil case.

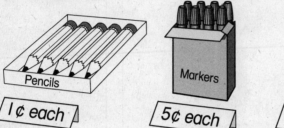

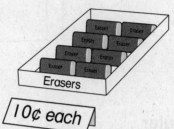

Pencils 1¢ each

Markers 5¢ each

Erasers 10¢ each

Pencil Case 1

total cost: _____

Pencil Case 2

total cost: _____

 Writing and Reasoning Describe a set of
4 items that costs more than 20¢. What is the total cost?

_____

_____

What Is the Missing Coin?

**Draw and label the coins listed.
Then draw the missing coin.**

1.	Jimmy has 2 quarters, 2 dimes, and another coin. He has 75¢ in all. What is the other coin?	missing coin
2.	Tisha has 1 half dollar, 1 nickel, and another coin. She has 65¢ in all. What is the other coin?	missing coin
3.	Ed has 1 quarter, 2 nickels, and another coin. He has 85¢ in all. What is the other coin?	missing coin

 Writing and Reasoning How did you find the missing coin in Exercise 3?

_____

_____

Arrange and Count Coins

Sort the coins by drawing them in the correct place in the chart below. Write the total value for each group of coins.

HALF DOLLAR	QUARTER	DIME	NICKEL	PENNY
50¢				
total value: ____¢	total value: ____¢	total value: ____¢	total value: ____¢	total value: ____¢

Writing and Reasoning Does the group with the greatest number of coins also have the greatest value? Explain.

_____

_____

Name _____

Sentence Patterns

**Complete each table. Use the pattern
to complete each sentence.**

1.

half dollars					5
nickels		20	30		

30 nickels have the same value as _____ half dollars.

2.

quarters	2				
_____		10	15		30

6 quarters have the same value as 30 _____.

3.

dimes	5			1
nickels		8	6	

8 nickels have the same value as _____ dimes.

Writing and Reasoning Explain how you knew
what coin name to write in the chart for Exercise 2.

_____

_____

_____

Make a Dollar

How much more money does each child need to buy the yo-yo? Draw the coins to solve.

$1.00

1. Ella has these coins.

_____

2. Brad has these coins.

_____

3. Garrett has these coins.

Writing and Reasoning Look at Exercise 3. Draw another set of coins that you could use to show the answer.

Name _____

What Time Is It?

**Read the clues. Write the time.
Draw the hour hand .**

1. The hour is an odd number. It is on an hour before 5:00. It is after 1:00. The time is _____. 	**2.** The time is half past an hour. The hour is an even number between 6 and 10. The time is _____. 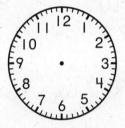
3. The hour is an even number. It is on an hour before 8:00. It is after 4:00. The time is _____. 	**4.** The time is half past an hour. The hour is an odd number between 7 and 11. The time is _____. 

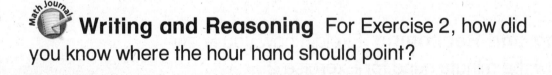 **Writing and Reasoning** For Exercise 2, how did you know where the hour hand should point?

_____

_____

_____

E97

Name _____

Missing Hands

**Read the sentence. Draw the hour hand
and the minute hand to show the time.**

1. Jack went to the library at 10:00.

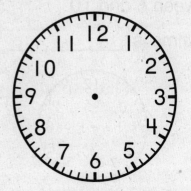

2. The movie started at 1:30.

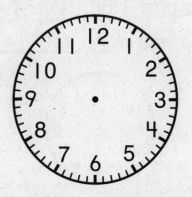

3. The race begins at 2:00.

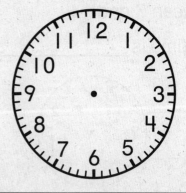

4. Joy went for a walk at 4:30.

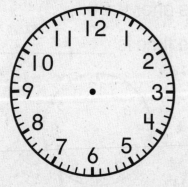

Writing and Reasoning Explain how you knew
where to draw the minute hand for Exercise 2.

_____

_____

_____

Name _____

Make It Match

Read the time on the digital clock. Draw the hour hand and the minute hand to show the same time on the analog clock.

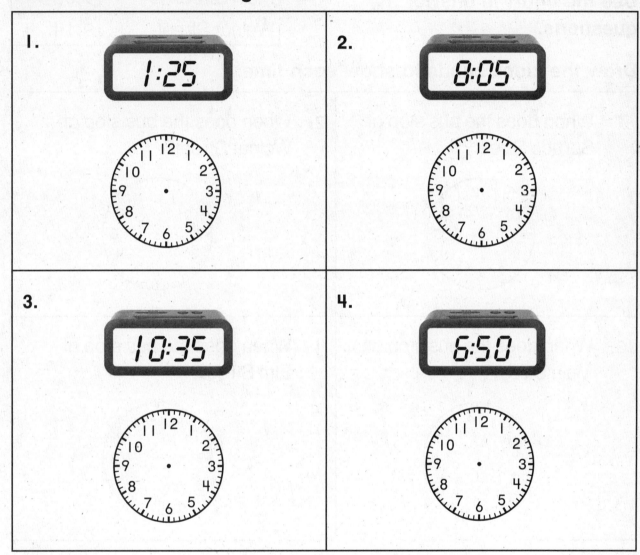

1. 1:25

2. 8:05

3. 10:35

4. 6:50

Writing and Reasoning How did you know where to draw the hour hand for Exercise 3? Explain.

_____

_____

_____

Name _____

On Time

The Oak City Bus stops at each street on the chart.

Use the chart to answer the questions.

Bus Stop Schedule	
Spruce Street	8:48
Elm Street	8:56
Main Street	9:03
Walnut Street	9:14

Draw the clock hands to show each time.

1. When does the bus stop at Spruce Street?

2. When does the bus stop at Walnut Street?

3. When does the bus stop at Main Street?

4. When does the bus stop at Elm Street?

Writing and Reasoning Explain how you knew where to draw the minute hand for Exercise 2.

_____

_____

_____

Name _____

How Much is the Same?

Complete the sentence.

Time Relationships
There are 60 minutes in 1 hour.
There are 24 hours in 1 day.
There are 7 days in 1 week.
There are about 4 weeks in 1 month.
There are 12 months in 1 year.

1. Mr. Davis works in his garden for 2 hours.
   How many minutes does he work in the garden?

   2 hours is the same as _____ minutes.

2. The art show is in 3 weeks. How many days
   until the art show?

   3 weeks is the same as _____ days.

3. The skating rink was closed for 4 days.
   How many hours was the skating rink closed?

   4 days is the same as _____ hours.

4. Susie's family lived on Park Street for 3 years.
   How many months did Susie's family live on Park Street?

   3 years is the same as _____ months.

 Writing and Reasoning Tell how you found the
answer for Exercise 3. _____

_____

_____

Name _____

Will It Stack?

Use these words to name the shapes.

sphere	rectangular prism	cylinder
cube	square pyramid	cone

Shape	Name of shape	Will the shape stack?
1.	_____	yes no
2.	_____	yes no
3.	_____	yes no
4.	_____	yes no
5.	_____	yes no

 Writing and Reasoning Describe when a shape can stack.

_____

_____

Picture Shapes

Use the directions to draw a picture.

1. Use the rectangle below to make a house.
   Draw a triangle above it for a roof.
2. Draw two hexagons for windows.
   Draw a quadrilateral for a door.
3. Draw a pentagon for a doghouse next to the house.
   Draw a quadrilateral for the opening to the doghouse.

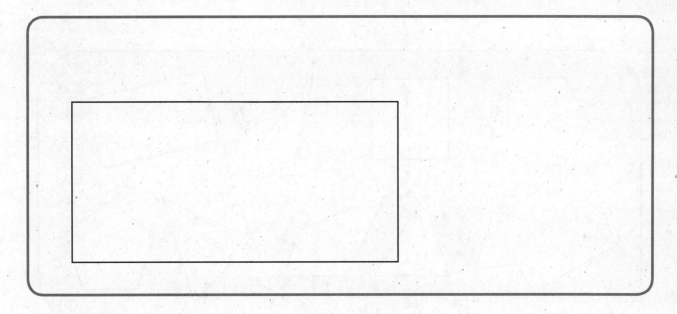

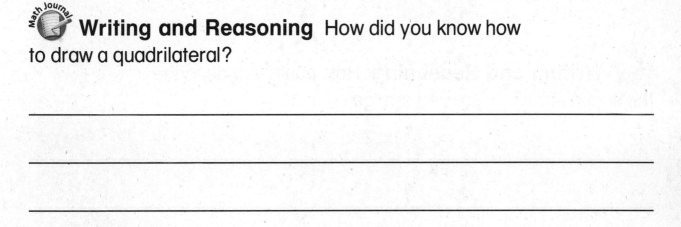

Writing and Reasoning How did you know how to draw a quadrilateral?

_____

_____

_____

Sort and Color

Find and color the shapes.

1. Find the quadrilaterals. Color them red.

2. Find the shapes with more than 5 sides. Color them yellow.

3. Find the shapes with fewer than 4 vertices. Color them blue.

4. Find the shapes that are left. Color them orange.

Writing and Reasoning How could you describe the shapes that you colored orange?

_____

_____

_____

Name _____

Matching Parts

Draw the matching part. The dashed line is a line of symmetry.

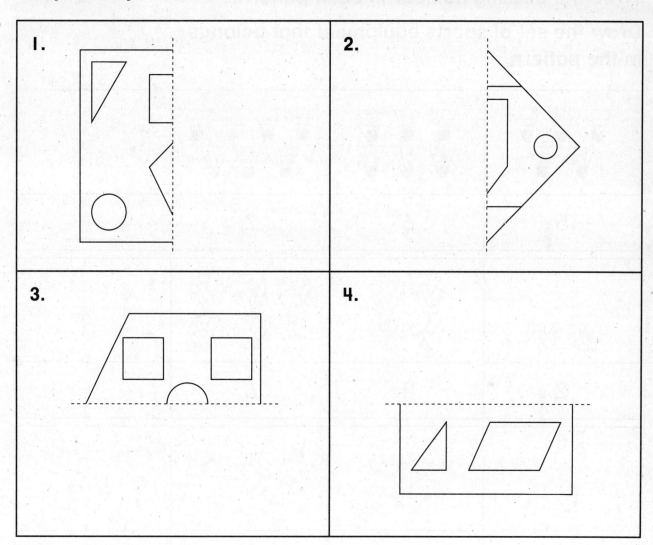

1.

2.

3.

4.

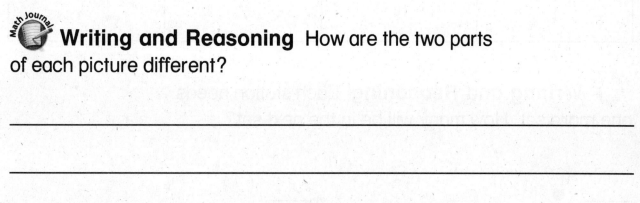

Writing and Reasoning How are the two parts of each picture different?

_____

_____

_____

Name _____

Field Day

The equipment for field day is in a pattern.

Write the missing number in each pattern.

Draw the set of sports equipment that belongs
in the pattern.

5	6	7	____

2	4	6	____

1	4	7	____

Writing and Reasoning Each station needs
one more set. How many will be in the next set?

____   ____   ____

Name _____

Circle Pattern

Mario wants to draw a pattern with circles. The number of circles changes by 3 from row to row. Draw the circles that could be in the first four rows of Mario's pattern.

1st row
2nd row
3rd row
4th row

Writing and Reasoning Draw the circles that should be in the 6th row of Mario's pattern.

Quilting Pattern

**Quilts often have shape patterns.
Draw 4 parts of a growing pattern
with the rule that is given.**

1. Rule: Add 3 triangles.

2. Rule: Add 4 circles.

3. Rule: Subtract 1 square.

4. Rule: Add 2 hearts.

Writing and Reasoning For Row 1, how many
triangles would be in the next 2 parts?

fifth part: _____ triangles   sixth part: _____ triangles

Pattern of Squares

**The first part of a growing pattern has
been drawn. Draw small squares to
show more parts in the pattern.**

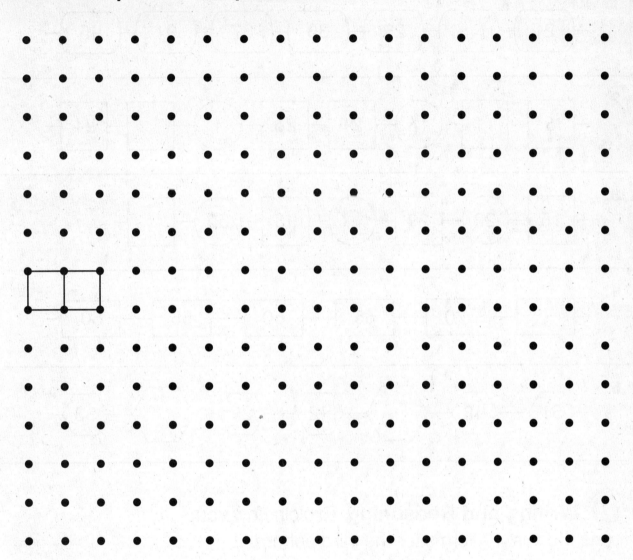

 Writing and Reasoning Describe a rule for this pattern.

_____

_____

_____

Name _____

Beaded Strings

Find the missing terms in each pattern.

1.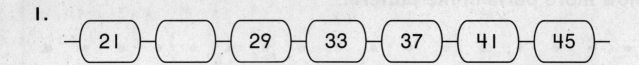

2.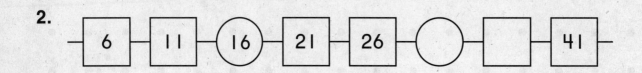

3.

4.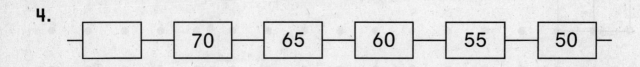

5.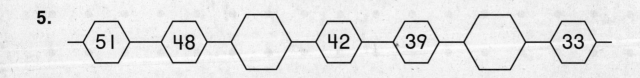

Writing and Reasoning Explain how you found the missing terms for the third pattern.

_____

_____

_____